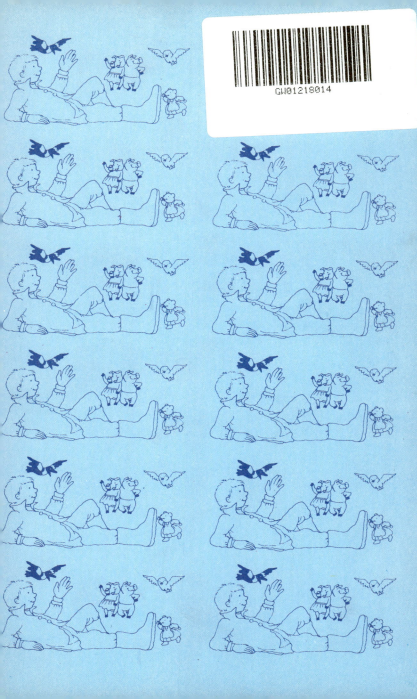

Barnabas is a lonely
giant who lives on his own,
that is until Owlie shows him
a way to make friends...

The Lonely Giant

A Bedtime Story

by Constance C Jones
illustrated by Gill Guile

Copyright © 1991 by World International Publishing Limited.
All rights reserved.
Published in Great Britain by World International Publishing Limited,
An Egmont Company, Egmont House, P.O.Box 111,
Great Ducie Street, Manchester M60 3BL.
Printed in DDR. ISBN 0 7498 0065 8

A CIP catalogue record for this book is available from the British Library

Barnabas was a lonely giant. He sat in his house and sighed. It was such a big sigh that his house trembled as though it sighed, too.

Owlie, who was very wise and lived in the tree at the side of Barnabas's house, called out to his friend, "What's the matter with you, Barnie?"

"Oh, Owlie, I am so miserable. I haven't a friend in the world."

"You've got me," said Owlie.

"But you are the only one who talks to me," said Barnie, sadly.

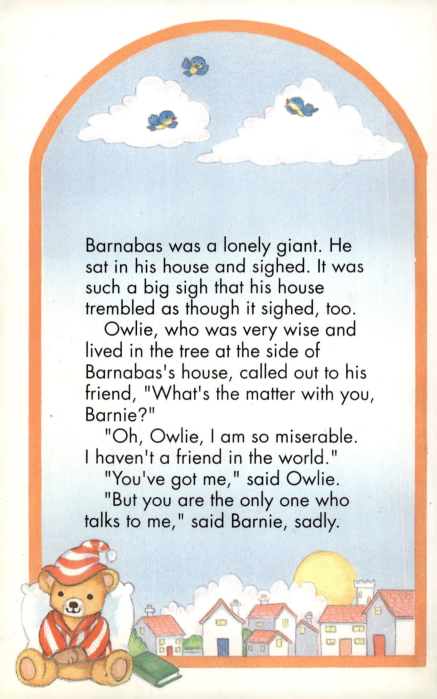

Owlie thought hard, then he said, "I'll tell you what, Barnie. Let me come and live with you for a while. That way I might be able to find out why no one makes friends with you."

"Oh, all right then," said Barnie. But he sounded so miserable that Owlie became quite cross with him.

"Well, don't sound so fed up. I am trying to help you, after all," said Owlie. "You must try and cheer yourself up, maybe that's why you don't have any friends."

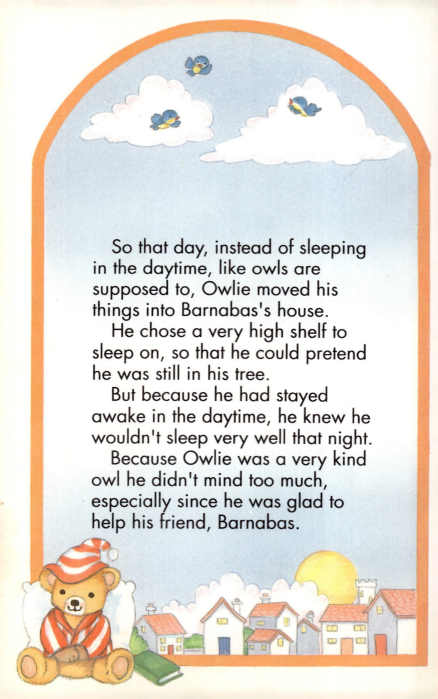

So that day, instead of sleeping in the daytime, like owls are supposed to, Owlie moved his things into Barnabas's house.

He chose a very high shelf to sleep on, so that he could pretend he was still in his tree.

But because he had stayed awake in the daytime, he knew he wouldn't sleep very well that night.

Because Owlie was a very kind owl he didn't mind too much, especially since he was glad to help his friend, Barnabas.

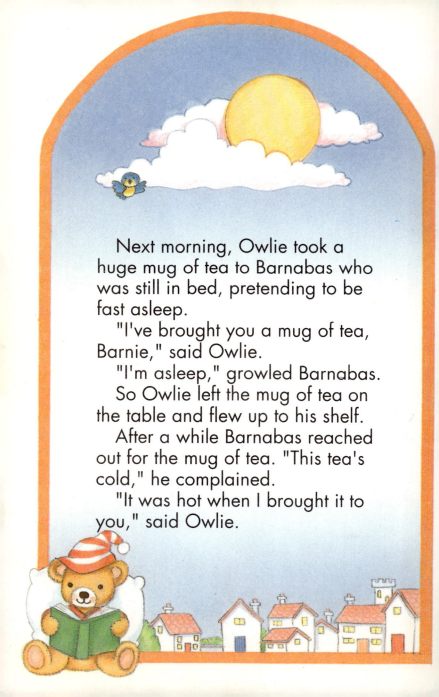

Next morning, Owlie took a huge mug of tea to Barnabas who was still in bed, pretending to be fast asleep.

"I've brought you a mug of tea, Barnie," said Owlie.

"I'm asleep," growled Barnabas.

So Owlie left the mug of tea on the table and flew up to his shelf.

After a while Barnabas reached out for the mug of tea. "This tea's cold," he complained.

"It was hot when I brought it to you," said Owlie.

Then Barnabas looked out of the window. "Oh look, it's raining," he grumbled.

"The grass and the flowers need rain," said Owlie.

"I never thought of that," said Barnabas.

"Now what are we going to do today?" asked Owlie.

"Do?" asked Barnie. "Why, nothing of course!"

"But doing nothing won't stop you from feeling lonely," said Owlie, trying to be helpful.

Barnabas didn't really like the idea of actually doing something. So he thought for a while, and then he said, "Well *you* think of something then."

Owlie had an idea. "Let's ask your neighbours to come for tea."

"Nobody ever comes to my house," said Barnabas, quietly.

"Do you ask them?" said Owlie.

"Of course not!" complained the lonely giant.

"Well, you will today!" said Owlie, looking pleased.

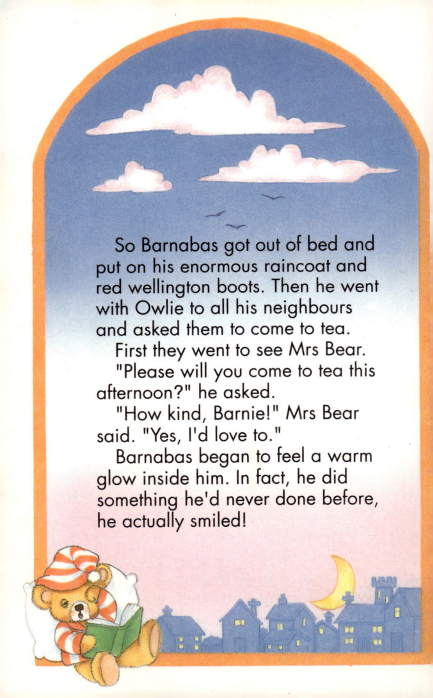

So Barnabas got out of bed and put on his enormous raincoat and red wellington boots. Then he went with Owlie to all his neighbours and asked them to come to tea.

First they went to see Mrs Bear.

"Please will you come to tea this afternoon?" he asked.

"How kind, Barnie!" Mrs Bear said. "Yes, I'd love to."

Barnabas began to feel a warm glow inside him. In fact, he did something he'd never done before, he actually smiled!

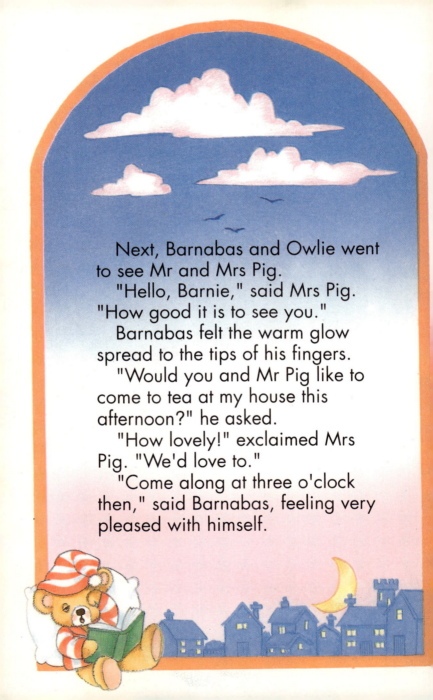

Next, Barnabas and Owlie went to see Mr and Mrs Pig.

"Hello, Barnie," said Mrs Pig. "How good it is to see you."

Barnabas felt the warm glow spread to the tips of his fingers.

"Would you and Mr Pig like to come to tea at my house this afternoon?" he asked.

"How lovely!" exclaimed Mrs Pig. "We'd love to."

"Come along at three o'clock then," said Barnabas, feeling very pleased with himself.

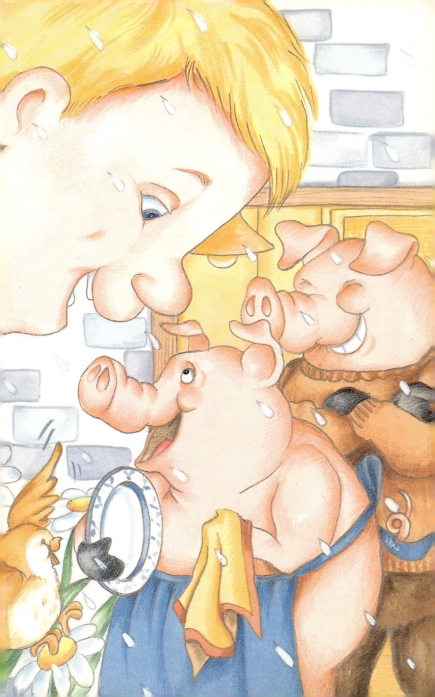

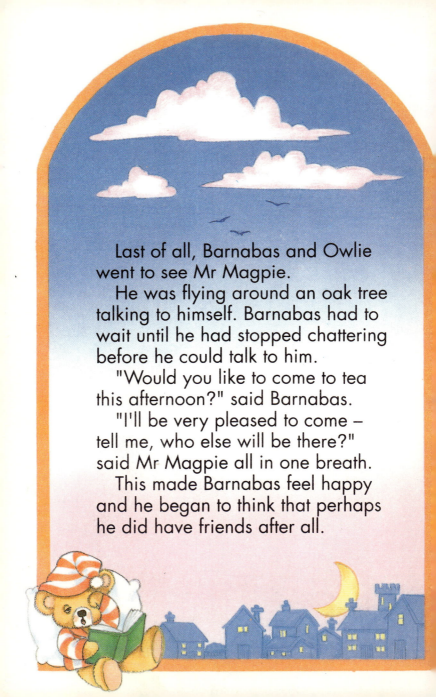

Last of all, Barnabas and Owlie went to see Mr Magpie.

He was flying around an oak tree talking to himself. Barnabas had to wait until he had stopped chattering before he could talk to him.

"Would you like to come to tea this afternoon?" said Barnabas.

"I'll be very pleased to come — tell me, who else will be there?" said Mr Magpie all in one breath.

This made Barnabas feel happy and he began to think that perhaps he did have friends after all.

Soon Barnabas and Owlie were back at home.

"Let's tidy the house and do some baking," said Owlie.

"I can't bake," said Barnabas.

"Have you ever tried?" asked Owlie. Barnabas shook his head.

Owlie took a book from the bookshelf. "This book will tell you how to bake things. Have a go at making scones," he said.

Barnabas read the book and soon the house was filled with the delicious smell of scones baking.

Barnabas cleaned the house and made it look as tidy as he could.

Then he set the table with a lovely white table cloth. He used the best plates and the best cutlery and everything soon looked wonderful.

Owlie watched Barnabas at work and could tell that he was enjoying every little bit of it.

When the scones were nearly baked, Owlie said, "Now we'll make some strawberry jam sandwiches."

At last it was three o'clock.
"I'm so excited," said Barnabas.
Then Mrs Bear, Mr and Mrs Pig and Mr Magpie arrived.

It was such a happy party. Everyone enjoyed themselves and soon all the scones and strawberry jam sandwiches had been eaten.

Barnabas felt happy and he couldn't stop smiling.

"You're all my friends," he said.

Everyone agreed they *were* his friends, and from then on Barnabas was no longer a lonely giant!

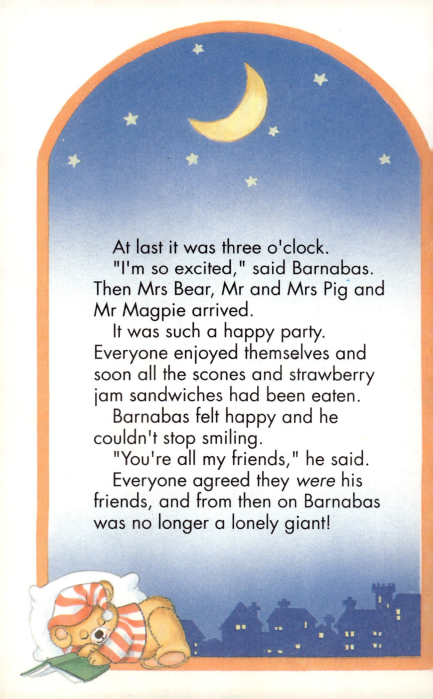

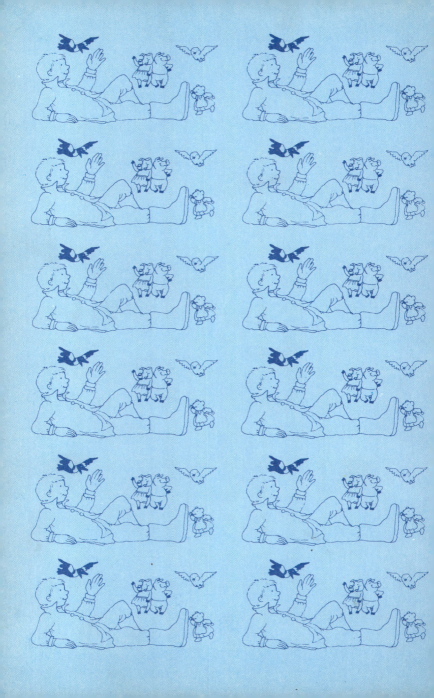